Dedicated to
Lata Patti & Narayan Thatha
who make all the amazing lemon cake and
tell stories that I could never have imagined.

Table of Countries

Colombia

Las Lajas Sanctuary is like a cathedral out of a fairy tale, as it sits on top of a deep river valley. Legend has it that a young woman and her deaf and mute daughter were able to stay here during a storm, and the Holy Virgin came to see them.

Fast Facts -
Location: Northern South America
Population: 49 million, or 3 Netherlands
Area: 707,686 sq. mi., or 7 New Zealands
Ethnic Groups: Mestizo and White (88%), Afro-Colombian (7%), Amerindian (4%)
Languages: Spanish (official), 65 Amerindian languages

Caribbean

Barranquilla
Cartagena
Darién Gulf
Panama
Cúcuta
Bucaramanga
Cauca
Magdalena
Medellín
Andes
Pacific Ocean
Buenaventura
Cordillera Occidental
Bogotá
Cordillera Oriental
Cali
Cordillera Central
Ibagué
Cordillera
Pasto
Ecuador
Amazon
Putumayo
Peru

Sea Colombia is the most biodiverse country in the world, with over 60,000 species! (including this little inca jay)

Zipaquirá Salt Cathedral is a cathedral that was built underground! It was a place where miners went to pray before going to work in the mines, and today is dazzlingy beautiful.

Tejo is a game in Colombia where instead of trying to throw a sack into a hole, you try to throw a disk onto a metal ring. If it lands, the disk explodes!

Venezuela Caño Cristales is a river that flows in southern Colombia. However, it is a rainbow colored river, as you can see yellow, green, black, and red too! This is caused by lots of colored plants, known as macarenia clavigera, that grow on the riverbed.

Meta

Orinoco Basin

Orinoco

Guaviare

Rainforest

Brazil

Caquetá

Food Corner:
Bandeja paisa is the national dish of Colombia. It has rice, minced meat, red beans, avocado, black pudding, or "morcella", chorizo (a type of sausage), and more, all in one dish!

Argentina

Fast Facts -
Location: Southern South America
Population: 47 million, or 1/3 of Japan
Area: 1,727,660 sq. mi., or 12 Japans
Ethnic Groups: European and Mestizo (97%), Amerindian (2%)
Languages: Spanish (official), Italian, English, German, Quechua, Guarani, and more.

The tango is a dance originating in Argentina and nearby Uruguay. The dance is said to be felt not by the feet, but by the "heart".

The current head of the Catholic Church, Pope Francis, is actually from Buenos Aires, Argentina!

Bolivia

Salta

Paraguay

Bermejo

Gran Chaco

Paraná

San Miguel de Tucumán

Salado

Chile

Andes

Córdoba

Pampas

Santa Fe

Uruguay

Brazil

Mendoza

Rosario

Uruguay

6

Buenos Aires

1

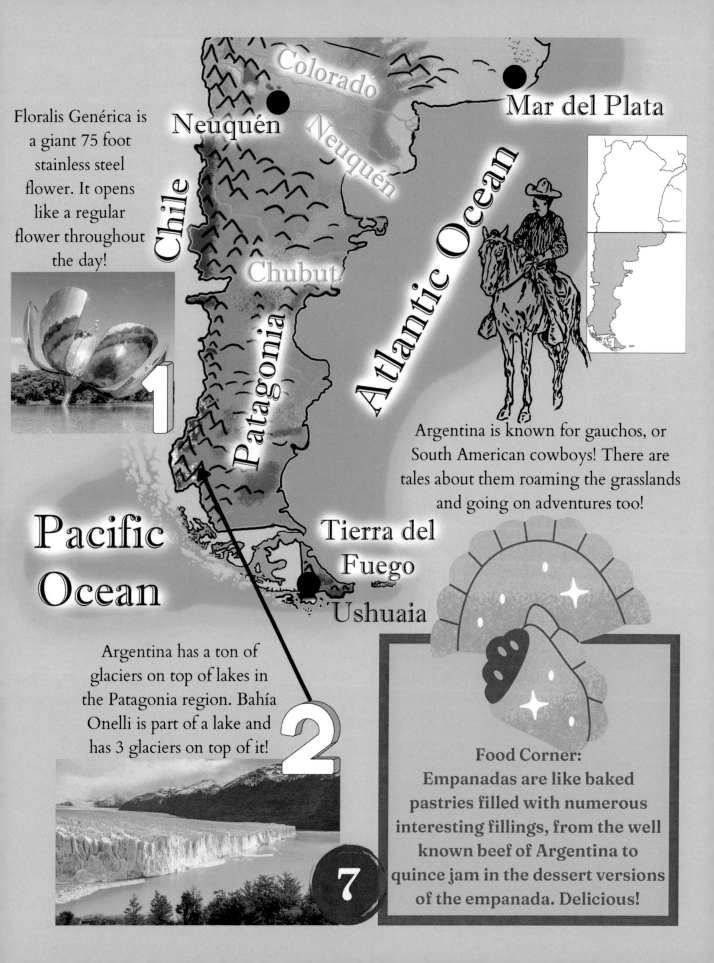

Floralis Genérica is a giant 75 foot stainless steel flower. It opens like a regular flower throughout the day!

1

Colorado

Neuquén

Neuquén

Chile

Chubut

Patagonia

Atlantic Ocean

Mar del Plata

Argentina is known for gauchos, or South American cowboys! There are tales about them roaming the grasslands and going on adventures too!

Pacific Ocean

Tierra del Fuego

Ushuaia

Argentina has a ton of glaciers on top of lakes in the Patagonia region. Bahía Onelli is part of a lake and has 3 glaciers on top of it!

2

7

Food Corner:
Empanadas are like baked pastries filled with numerous interesting fillings, from the well known beef of Argentina to quince jam in the dessert versions of the empanada. Delicious!

France

2 **3**

What else is built by Gustave Eiffel? Go to Book 1, page 5!

1

The Eiffel Tower is a renowned landmark. Built by French architect Gustave Eiffel, the tower actually gets 7 inches taller in the summer and 6 inches shorter in the winter because of the iron expanding and contracting!

United Kingdom

Lille

English Channel

Paris

Seine

Brest

Normandie

Bretagne

Atlantic Ocean

Nantes

Loire

Bour-gogne

Bay of Biscay

Aquitanie

Central Massif

Bordeaux

Garonne

Toulouse

Gascogne

Pyrénées

Spain

Andorra (tiny country)

Fast Facts -
Location: Western Europe
Population: 69 million, or 7 Greeces
Area: 400,039 sq. mi., or 3 Italys
Ethnic Groups: Celtic and Latin, many more minority communities.
Languages: French, others.

France has over 1500 types of cheese, including the pungent Roquefort, or blue cheese.

The croissant is a French pastry

Paris is known as the "City of Love" for the romantic vibes it exudes, from it's quaint les boulangeries (bakeries) to the Eiffel Tower!

The Louvre is the largest museum in the world, at 652,300 square feet, or 139 basketball courts! It also has almost 500,000 works of art, including the Mona Lisa.

2

Belgium

Luxembourg

Strasbourg

Rhin

Saône

Germany

The baguette is an integral part of French culture. There is even a law that says this bread can only be made with flour, salt, water, and yeast!

Switzerland

3

Lyon

Alps

Rhône

Italy

Nice

Marseille

Monaco (tiny country)

Tyrrhenian Sea

Corsica

Mediterranean Sea **9**

Food Corner:
Escargot is a well-known French delicacy. Served with a slice of bread on the side, this dish is stuffed with parsley and garlic butter. But what is the actual dish? Snails!

Ukraine

12

Belarus

Polesian Lowland

Desna

Poland

Lviv

Kyiv

Dnieper Upland

Podolian Upland

Dniester

Buh

3

Slovakia

Carpathian Mts.

Hungary

Romania

Moldova

Mykolayiv

Odesa

Romania

Ukrainian pysanky eggs are like Easter Eggs, but they have intricate, beautiful designs on top too!

Fast Facts -
Location: Eastern Europe
Population: 43 million, or 8 Singapores
Area: 233,032 sq. mi, or 20 Belgiums
Ethnic Groups: Ukrainian (78%), Russian (17%), others
Languages: Ukrainian (official), Russian, others

Ukraine was invaded by Russia in 2022. Ukrainians have valiantly fought back to retake their country.

10

Black Sea

1 On April 26, 1986, a nuclear power plant exploded in Chernobyl. To this day, humans cannot live near the area of the disaster because they will get radiation sickness.

2 St. Sophia's Cathedral is a magnificent cathedral built over 1000 years ago under the reign of King Yaroslav the Wise. He was from the Kievan Rus, which at it's height was 5.5 United Kingdoms in size!

Palanok Castle has a deep and dark reputation. A princess held off the invading Austrian army for 3 years. Then, the castle served as a prison. Also, its on top of a volcano!

3

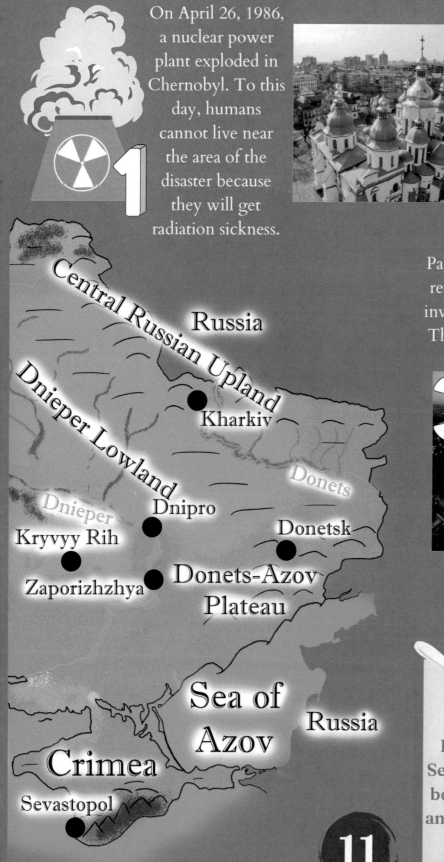

Russia

Central Russian Upland

Dnieper Lowland

Kharkiv

Donets

Dnieper

Dnipro

Kryvyy Rih

Donetsk

Zaporizhzhya

Donets-Azov Plateau

Sea of Azov

Russia

Crimea

Sevastopol

11

Food Corner:
Borscht is a tangy red soup. Served hot or cold, it has meat, beetroot, cabbages, tomatoes, and more! It is also served with garlic buns known as pampushky. Healthy and tasty!

South Africa

Table Mountain is one of the most iconic landmarks of not only South Africa, but Africa too! It has a ton of species that live only on this mountain, or endemic species, at 2200 in total!

Nelson Mandela was the father of South Africa. He peacefully brought down the Apartheid government that segregated Whites from Blacks, and during the resistance, he was imprisoned for 27 years!

1

Fast Facts -
Location: Southern Africa
Population: 58 million, or 19 Denmarks
Area: 757,507 sq. mi., or 25 South Koreas
Ethnic Groups: Black African (81%), Mixed Race (9%), White (8%), Asian (2%)
Language: isiZulu, Afrikaans, English (used by most), all official with 8 other official languages.

1

Kalahari Desert

Namibia

Orange

Namaqualand

Great Karoo

Doring

Draken

Atlantic Ocean

Little Karoo

Cape Town

South Africa grows the most macadamia nuts in the world! Who knows, maybe the macadamia nuts in your cupboard are from South Africa!

Tugela Falls is the second highest waterfall in the world, at more than 3000 feet. That is more than 10 times the height of the Statue of Liberty!

2

Zimbabwe

Botswana

Limpopo

Transvaal

Mozambique

Polokwane

Olifants

Drakensburg Mts.

Eswatini

Pretoria

Johannesburg

Vereeniging

Vaal

The Sudwala Caves are the oldest caves in the world, being over 240 million years old. That is the same period as when the dinosaurs first started to appear on Earth!

3

Kimberley

Bloemfontein

Lesotho

Durban

2

...sburg Mts.

Sondags

Indian Ocean

East London

Gqeberha

13

Food Corner:
Biltong is a type of meat jerky made by the indigenous people of South Africa, and is cured with coriander, pepper, salt, and spices, and has a low fat content. Yum!

Tanzania

The Serengeti Plains have a giant migration of 1.5 million wildebeest and 250,000 zebra across the plains. Combined, that is more animals than 2 San Francisco's worth of people!

1 Rwanda

Burundi

Democratic Republic of the Congo

Uganda

Lake Victoria

4

2

Serengeti Plains

Mwanza

Arusha

Maasai Steppe

East African Rift

Kigoma-Ujiji

Gombe

Great Rift Valley

West African Rift

Lake Tanganyika

5

Dodoma

Great Ruaha

Udzungwa Mts.

Mbeya

Zambia

Songea

Lake Malawi

Malawi

Mozam-bique

Fast Facts -
Location: Eastern Africa
Population: 66 million, or 13 Irelands
Area: 588,625 sq. mi., or 2 Italys
Ethnic Groups: Mainland - African (99%), Other (1%). Zanzibar - Arab, African, Mixed.
Language: Kiswahili (official), English (official), Arabic (used on Zanzibar)

Tanzania is actually a combination of 2 different countries, Tanganyika (green), and Zanzibar (Unguja and Pemba Islands, purple). Eventually, they merged, forming the **Tan**ganika-**Zan**zibar-**ia** we know today!

Mt. Kilimanjaro is the tallest mountain in Africa, at almost 20,000 feet tall! Furthermore, the mountain is right next to the Equator, which is deep in the tropics, but even then, the peak is cold enough to have glaciers!

This is Mtoni Palace of the Sultanate of Zanzibar. Though it was destroyed, and the sultanate abolished, at it's height, it was part of the Kingdom of Oman, which was over 2000 miles away!

Kenya

Tanga

Pemba

Dar es Salaam

Unguja

Zanzibar

Morogoro

Indian Ocean

Rufiji

Ruvuma

In Tanzania, Lake Victoria is the second largest freshwater lake in the world, and Lake Tanganyika is the second oldest and second deepest lake in the world! Those are some giant lakes!

Lake Tanganyika

Food Corner:
Kuku paka is a dish that fuses African, Arabic, and Indian cuisines to make a unique Tanzanian dish. It is chicken dunked in a creamy coconut sauce, often eaten with rice. Yum!

4 Lake Victoria

15

5

Israel

1

The Western Wall, located in Jerusalem is one of the holiest sites for the Jewish religion. Interestingly, of the 45 rows of stone, 17 are underground!

The Dome of the Rock is a shrine that is sacred to Muslims, Jews, and Christians, as many important events in the 3 religions have occurred here at the rock which this shrine houses.

2

Fast Facts -
Location: Western Asia
Population: 9 million, or 1.6 Norways
Area: 13,631 sq. mi., or a little smaller than Switzerland
Ethnic Groups: Jewish 74%, Arab, 21%, others 5%

Language: Hebrew (official), Arabic, English

Mediterranean

16

Lebanon

Golan Heights (disputed)

Syria

Ḥefa

Galilee

Sea of Galilee

Nābulus

Tel Aviv-Yafo

West

Jordan

Sea **Bank**

Jerusalem   Dead

Ashqelon   Sea

Gaza   Al Khalıl

Gaza Strip

Khān Yūnis   Be'er Sheva   Jordan

1,2 and **3**

are all in Jerusalem.

Egypt   **Negev Desert**

4

3

Elat   Gulf of Aqaba

The Church of the Holy Sepulchre is one of the most holy sites in Christianity, as it is where Jesus was crucified. There is actually a glass window at the top of the Church, which often has sunlight streaming into the church.

The Dead Sea is the lowest point on earth – at about 400 meters or 1200 yards below sea level. Furthermore, the Dead Sea is super salty, and a result of this salinity is that you can float on the sea without even trying!

The voice mail was invented in Israel in the late 1990s!

17

Food Corner:
Hummus is a dip that is often had with middle eastern food. It is made of mashed chickpeas and topped with tahini, olive oil, and more. That sounds really tasty!

Turkey

The Hagia Sophia, is a magnificent building. It was built in the 300s A.D. For 1000 years, it was a church, before being converted into a mosque in the 1400s, and finally into a museum in the 1900s.

1

Black

Bulgaria

Thrace
İstanbul
Sea of Marmara

Saint Nicholas, otherwise known as Santa Claus, was actually born in Turkey; specifically Patara, Turkey.

Bursa

Sakarya

Köroglu Mts.

Ankara

Anatolian Plateau

Lake Tuz

Gediz

Aegean Sea

İzmir

Büyük-Menderes

Konya

Antalya

Toros Mts.

Mersin

2

Mediterranean Sea

Fast Facts -
Location: Western Asia
Population: 83 million, or 8 Portugals
Area: 486,883 sq. mi., or 13 Irelands
Ethnic Groups: Turkish 70-75%, Kurdish, 19%, Others 6-11%
Languages: Turkish (official), Kurdish, Others

18

Turkey is one of the few countries that spans 2 continents! The red part is in Europe, and the blue part is in Asia.

The Ottoman Empire was a powerful empire that lasted for over 600 years. Ruled by a Sultan, the empire spanned from North Africa all the way to southern Russia!

Sea

Georgia

Kuzey Anadolu Mts.

Armenia

Aras

Kızılırmak

Euphrates

Armenian Highlands

Azerbaijan

Murat

Iran

Cappadocia

Diyarbakır

Lake Van

Adana

Gaziantep

Sanlıurfa

Tigris

Iraq

Syria

The Cappadocia Fairies are rock formations in the shape of chimneys. Under these fairy chimneys however, there are actually underground dwellings used by Christians who at the time were persecuted.

Food Corner:
Baklava is a popular dish of the Middle East, but Turkey is the best known for it. Thin layers of pastry covered in syrup with pistachios, it is something not to miss!

Kazakhstan

Khoja Ahmed Yassawi Mausoleum honors the first Central Asian poet, Khoja Ahmed Yasawi, who lived in the 1100s A.D. It was ordered to be built by the emperor Timur, ruler of the large Timurid Empire, in the 13th century.

1

Russia

Oral

Zhayyq

Aqtöbe

Caspian Depression

Atyraū

Kazakh

Torghay Valley

Caspian Sea

Aral Sea

Syr Darya

Turan Lowland Uzbekistan

4

Turkmenistan

Fast Facts -
Location: Central Asia
Population: 20 million, or 2 Swedens
Area: 1,693,174 sq. mi., or 3 Irans
Ethnic Groups: Kazakh (70%), Russian (18%), Uzbek (3%), Other (9%).
Languages: Kazakh, Russian

20

The apple originates from the slopes of the mountains near Almaty, Kazakhstan!

2

Bayterek Tower is a landmark of the capital, Astana. Built in 2002, it has a giant glass sphere that weighs almost 300 tons, or over 150 cars!

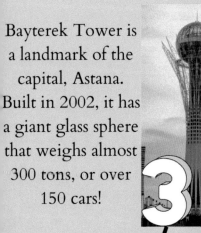

3

Sherkala Mountain is quite an interesting place. Literally meaning "Lion's Fortress", to climb the mountain, one has to go through a tunnel. And if that's not adventure enough, at the top one can explore the ruins of the fortress built by Dzhunga, Genghis Khan's son.

4

Horses may have first been domesticated and ridden in Kazakhstan, and are a large part of the Kazakh steppe culture.

Ertis (Irtysh)

Russia

Esil

Astana

Steppe

Semey

Altay Mts.

Öskemen

Qaraghandy

Kazakh Uplands

Betpaqdala Desert

Balqash Lake

China

1

Almaty

2

Taraz

Tian Shan

Shymkent

Kyrgyzstan

21

Food Corner:
Baursak is the Kazakh equivalent of doughnuts! Legend has it that the fragrant smell of the doughnuts goes up to heaven so the deceased can get this little treat! In 2014, a Guinness world record was set, with 856 pounds of baursak being made, or the weight of 6 King sized beds!

Vietnam

Ha Long Bay is one that is filled with tall, rocky islands peaking out of the water to create a stunning sight. Dispersed among these, one can find water filled caves and a bunch of villages floating on water.

China

Hoang Lien Son Range

Lo

Da (Black)

Hong River Delta

Hanoi

Hong (Red)

Haiphong

Laos

Ca

Gulf of Tonkin

Vinh

The water puppets of Vietnam are little puppets that are used to tell fables of northern Vietnam's village life like duck herding and rice planting, but on a stage filled with water!

1

2

Day Truong Son Mts.

Hue

Da Nang

Fast Facts -
Location: Southeast Asia
Population: 105 million, or 2 Italys
Area: 127,881 sq. mi., or 3 South Koreas
Ethnic Groups: Kinh (85%), Tay (2%), Thai (2%), Others (11%).
Languages: Vietnamese (official), English

The Cu Chi Tunnels were built during the Vietnam War, a tough war between Vietnam and the U.S.A. During the war, the North Vietnamese had to build tiny tunnels, like the one shown.

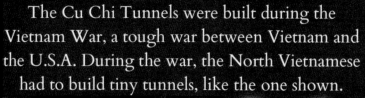

3

Cambodia

Qui Nhon

Di Linh Plateau

Nha Trang

Mekong

Hau

Bien Hoa

Ho Chi Minh

Can Tho

Mekong Delta

South China Sea

Vietnam has the most ducks, with 27% of the world's ducks!

The Imperial City at Hue was the residence of the kings of the Nguyen dynasty, who ruled up till 1945. The palace has been well restored, and is a beautiful place to see.

2

23

Food Corner:
Banh khot is a little crispy bite sized savory pastry. It includes a little crispy, cup-shaped pastry that can be topped with anything from shrimp to quail's egg! On top of that, it is served with lettuce, mint, basil, and more herbs!

Geogractivities

Identify the Countries:

1. Santa Claus is from this country!

_____

2. The current pope, Pope Francis, is from this country!

_____

3. This country may have been the first place where horses were domesticated!

_____

4. The oldest caves in the world can be found here!

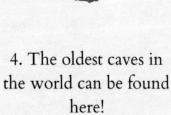

_____

4. This country has holy sites for Jews, Christians, and Muslims!

_____

24

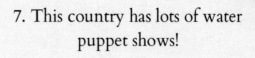

7. This country has lots of water puppet shows!

_____

6. This country is the most biodiverse in the world, with over 60,000 species!

_____

8. This country has beautifully decorated pysanky eggs!

_____

9. This country has 2 giant lakes – Lake Victoria and Lake Tanganyika!

10. This country's capital is known as the City of Love!

_____

_____

Fill in the Crossword:

26

Hints:

Across:

1. This country is where apples originated!
2. This country has a migration of 1.5 million wildebeest and 250,000 zebras!
3. The Ottoman Empire, an empire lasting over 600 years, was from here.
4. This country has foods like the baguette, croissant, and escargot!
5. This country has a game where when disks are thrown to hit metal rings, the disks explode!

Down:

1. This country has the castle which was a prison, had a story of a brave princess, and is on top of a volcano!
2. Gauchos, or South American cowboys, can be found here.
3. This country has more than a quarter of the world's ducks!
4. The macadamia nuts in your cupboard may be from this country.
5. The voicemail was made here!

Guess the Country from the Image (Challenge):

1._____

2._____

3._____

4._____

28

5._____

6._____

7._____

8._____

9._____

10._____

Answers:

Identify the Countries by Their Flag:

1. Turkey
2. Argentina
3. Kazakhstan
4. Israel
5. South Africa
6. Colombia
7. Vietnam
8. Ukraine
9. Tanzania
10. France

Fill in the Crossword:

Across –
1. Kazakhstan
2. Tanzania
3. Turkey
4. France
5. Colombia

Down –
1. Ukraine
2. Argentina
3. Vietnam
4. South Africa
5. Israel

Guess the Country from the Image:

1. Tanzania
2. Israel
3. France
4. Vietnam
5. Argentina
6. Colombia
7. Kazakhstan
8. South Africa
9. Ukraine
10. Turkey

30

Acknowledgements:

Geography is my energy. Actually, my parents and grandparents, and people I am with are the people who provide me with energy. Geography is the gas pedal. My grandparents are amazing. From the lemon cakes to the undelved-into stories, Lata Patti and Narayan Thatha are some of the best people I could ask for in my life. And all of the children I was able to talk to, you guys brought so much joy to my life. And of course, to end this off: Mom, Dad, and Moose - You guys are everything.

Made in the USA
Middletown, DE
16 October 2023